Christopher Shippy G.Canton

MW00960828

# Big Chris & Krosby
# Take Hawaii

Christopher Shippy G.Canton

Inspired by my daughter Krosby & the good people at
**Mauna Kea Luau**
Honolulu, Hawaii
2023

Big Chris and his daughter Krosby, took a very long flight,
Over the ocean they flew, long into the night.

Paradise was not far away, Honolulu was clearly in their sight,
Big Chris peeked through the window and saw the glow of sunlight.

The pilot started speaking in a low baritone voice,
He said all the passengers can begin to deboard and Krosby started to rejoice.

Big Chris grabbed his bag, and he took Krosby's too,
They started walking together when they noticed the airline's crew.

They greeted us all with a big happy smile and placed a lei over their heads,
Big Chris glanced over at Krosby and saw a tear from her eye did shed.

They walked down the jetway and towards the baggage claim,

When out of nowhere Krosby heard someone call out her name.


She looked down the lane and back behind her too,

But she saw no one, and she didn't have a clue.


Just then a lady ran up and said "Hi If you're Big Chris & Krosby

I'm here to pick you up!"

She then presented both with another lei made of Buttercup.


The sign on the wall said, "Welcome to Hawaii, we hope you're stay

is great!"

"Aloha to all of you to the USA's 50th State."

They walked downstairs to ground transportation, where a TownCar was standing by,

Giddy with excitement, they both leapt in the back, and staired up to the sky.


Off they were to the Hotel Princess, the gem of all hotels,

They looked through the back window and to the airport, bid farewell.

That first day on the Island of Oahu, they took a dinner cruise,

Crab, steak, and chicken adorned their dinner plate, sitting by the window,

taking in the views.


The water crashing on the rocks, people surfing waves,

Both knew they could stay here not for just a few hours, but certainly for days.


With their plates cleaned up, not a morsal left to devour,

The captain came to their table and gifted them a flower.


Pink and yellow in color, most likely was a hibiscus,

They were taking it all in and with so much to discuss.


They whispered to one another of what an incredible night they'd had,

Krosby was so excited, so thankful for her dad.

Once the cruise was over and the entertainment all wrapped up,

Big Chris and Krosby took one last sip from their fancy coconut cup.


They walked off the ship, sharing stories of what they'd seen,

Admiring all the trees and bushes with their beautiful shades of green.


Off to a market that was not too far away,

They grabbed a couple snacks the following day.

The next day came and with so much more to see,

Big Chris and Krosby jumped out of bed and headed out to sea.


There it was, the Northern Pacific Ocean, soft sand, and clear blue water,

The local women were sharing a dance and to Krosby they made an offer.


"Come here little one, learn to dance the Hula,

It is a native Hawaiian dance that was performed for King Kalakaua".


Formal dress is required, no grass skirts for this dance,

Leis for their head were made by hand, all from local plants.

Christopher Shippy G.Canton

Hula is a slow dance accompanied by the beat of a drum,

It takes years and years of practice, so a professional you'll become.


To dance the hula, takes great strength and grace,

Slow movements with your arms and hips with a smile on your face.

Another part of hula that makes it so enjoyable to observe,

Is the chant or oli as they call it which helps to preserve,

this incredible history of a culture from so long ago,

Where the significance of a specific fruit is dire, they call it a nee-oo

(Niu)

From the Cocos Nucifera , the mainlanders call it a coconut tree,

Each part of the palm is used including the trunk, shells, and leaves.

Native Hawaiians drink the milk, makes plates, bowls, and baskets,

Big Chris wonders if they could even make a jacket?

After the hula lesson ended, many hugs were exchanged,

Off for some incredible Island hopping that Big Chris had arranged.


Onward to the Manoa Falls Trails, and sightseeing along the way,

Big Chris surprised Krosby with a beautiful bouquet.

Up the hill and towards the mountain top,

The trees were incredible and seemed to never stop.

Different trees than way back home from where Big Chris and Krosby came,

Hardly two were just alike, nothing was the same.

Christopher Shippy G.Canton

Magnificent trees that had climbed higher than the skies,

The Banyan and the Koa gave them quite a big surprise.


The Banyan isn't just tall but also very broad,

Its amazing rooting system left them both slack-jawed.


Amazing isn't quite enough to express these tree's incredible beauty

Mangos, citrus & avocados trees also provide Hawaiians with something fruity.

After the drive was done and Big Chris and Krosby were content,

They headed back to their hotel to rest and to lament.


After some rest and a hamburger or two,

Big Chris and Krosby got in the car and headed to their lu'au, debut.


An hours' drive away from Honolulu, on Kamehameha Highway,

Big Chris and Krosby spotted a rainbow nature put on display.


They ooh'd and aah'd and counted the colors.

which made the optical phenomenon,

Don't take too long to look though for soon it will be gone.


It was magical, mystical, even supernatural,

Strange in appearance but so incredibly fantastical.

Off the highway they veered, farms now on either side,

Sugarcane fields and more Banyan trees, the perfect place to hide.


Soon they arrived and were welcomed like royalty,

This their first lu'au, Welcome to Mauna Kea

Down the path they walked, not knowing where to look,

They came upon a table to add their names into a book.


Big Chris wrote his name and added Krosby's too,

When to their right they noticed a welcome table offering a tray of pū-pū.


Pū-pū is an appetizer, relish or hors d'oeuvre,

Usually not brought to you, this food is all self-serve.


Big Chris and Krosby took a plate of tiny bite-sized food,

Boiled peanuts, sashimi, and a serving of edamame too.

They grabbed their drinks and stopped for a moment to take in the
view,

They turned their attention to a woman teaching how to use Bamboo,

to make a fan, a mat a knife and even a pen or two.


Krosby then purchased a flower clip that she'd place in her hair,

Yellow, her favorite color, she wore it everywhere.

Big Chris and Krosby then took their seat,

Soon eyeing the buffet tables lined with delicious meat.


Fish and pulled pork, sticky rice, and purple bread,

Truly there was sufficient to make sure everyone was fed.

After eating and talking to the couple who shared the communal table,

Big Chris finished and wanted more but just wasn't able.


Just then the show began, a kahiko* and the ancient hula,

With inspiration from Laka, a goddess, an ancient akua**.


Slowly swaying hips and hands to express an idea,

hula is a dance shared around the world, even in South Korea!

---

*kahiko - traditional dances that combined with oli (chants), percussion instruments like Pa'u, and specifically coordinated movements that tell stories of different people, places, and events.

**A supernatural being

Then came the fire dancers, what a show to remember,

Lighting up the sky with fire and floating embers.

The art of fire dancing, originated by the Polynesians,

was adopted quickly by the Maori Warriors from the country of New Zealand.

Poi is a Maori word meaning "ball on a string."

These warriors used it for training and exercise, in order to protect the King.

The Samoans adopted this tradition, to tempt others to a fight,

Using a fireknife, a 14-inch blade, there were no guns used in sight.

Soon the show was over, and it was time to part ways,

with our new friends from across the table, but we all wanted to stay.

Big Chris and Krosby jumped walk over to the car they'd rented,

To make the trek back to the hotel, and relive the memories, so unprecedented.

Friday morning came so fast, but there was so much more to do,

On their way to their next adventure, a tunnel they went through.

Off to Pearl Harbor, the scene of so much sorrow,

For all those who lost their lives, wishing they could still see tomorrow.

Museums and artifacts from that fateful day to see,

The place of death and destruction, so much pain and agony.

Big Chris and Krosby, read the info plastered on the walls,

And discussed the carnage that happened the day the Fleet would fall.

So sad the lives which were lost and, in their honor, do we say,

To you noble servicemen, for you we will pray

for solace for your family and for your souls still in motion,

As your bodies lie peacefully at the bottom of the Northern Pacific Ocean.


As the day wears on and they leave this sacred ground,

A renewed spirit of Patriotism for both of them was found.


A salute, a last look over the shoulder,

Walking away feeling a wiser, and just a little bit older.

USS Arizona survivors. (from top left) Raymond Haerry, Lou Conter, Donald Stratton, Clare Hetrick, Ken Potts, Lauren Bruner, Joe Langdell, Lonnie Cook and John Anderson

Arizona Republic, 2014

The final day in Hawaii, where will Big Chris and Krosby go?

To the famous Lanikai beach, once called Ka'ohao.


Spectacular views and breathtaking scenery,

Sandy beach, views of the Mokes, all with so much greenery.


Time to take a respite, to sit and take in what the universe has created,

No touch from a human hand, an area just naturally created..


Lanikai, Hawaiian for Heavenly Sea,

To sit and look out at the ocean, and all its nature-made beauty.

Watch out for the Portuguese Man-of-War* or the Stinging Limu,**

One touch from one of these will leave your feet black and blue.


*Jellyfish

**Seaweed

The day goes by, more perfect it could not have been,

For this daddy-daughter team, they'll surely return again,

to witness again the wonders and beauty that make up the Aloha state,

In a month or maybe just next year, the thing that is known for sure, is they simply cannot wait.

To my incredible daughter Krosby,

I have loved you since before time began.

I enjoy our time together; I'll take any that I can.

This trip, just you and me, will live within my heart until the sun fades away,

'till the last moonlight, the last sunray.

Made in the USA
Las Vegas, NV
27 October 2023

79816416R00033